# STAR WARS
## THE FORCE AWAKENS
# HEAD-TO-HEAD

# 30 ALL-NEW MATCHUPS THE GALAXY HAS NEVER SEEN!

BY PABLO HIDALGO

**SCHOLASTIC**

an imprint of

**SCHOLASTIC**

www.scholastic.com

This edition published by Scholastic Inc., 557 Broadway, New York, NY 10012 by arrangement with becker&mayer!. Scholastic and associated logos are trademarks and/or registered trademarks of Scholastic Inc.

Scholastic Inc., New York, NY

Scholastic Canada Ltd., Markham, Ontario

Produced by becker&mayer!
11120 NE 33rd Place, Suite 101
Bellevue, WA 98004
www.beckermayer.com

becker&mayer!
BOOK PRODUCERS

If you have questions or comments about this product, please visit www.beckermayer/customerservice and click on Customer Service Request Form.

Edited by Delia Greve

Designed by Scott Richardson

Production management by Cindy Curren

Design Elements: Page 1: Metal background © Sirirat Dechmon/Shutterstock. Page 2: Metal background © Ensuper/Shutterstock. Page 3: © Ensuper/Shutterstock. Page 4-63: Abstract data © pixelparticle/Shutterstock; Glass plate © Jack1e/Shutterstock; Black frame © Aleksandr Bryliaev/Shutterstock; Transparent glass frame © Aleksandr Bryliaev/Shutterstock; Abstract polygon © molaruso/Shutterstock; Metal background © Sirirat Dechmon/Shutterstock; Night sky © nienora/Shutterstock; rusty metal © schankz/Shutterstock; metal background © schankz/Shutterstock; The California Nebula © Albert Barr/Shutterstock; The Flaming Star Nebula © Albert Barr/Shutterstock; Peeled blue wall © Marc Bruxelle/Shutterstock; Metal surface with cracked paint © Fotokor77/Shutterstock. Page 64: Metal background © Ensuper/Shutterstock.

Printed, manufactured, and assembled in Jefferson City, MO

First printing, January 2016

10 9 8 7 6 5 4 3 2 1          16 17 18 19 20/0

ISBN 978-0-545-93096-3

470187  1/16

15341

The Force awakens with the power to create the possible and impossible. As heroes, villains, creatures, and vehicles from across generations square off, let your imagination–along with the provided stats, skills, and details–give these incredible duels shape and help you decide who will win. Compare your predictions with the experts' rulings on the last page.

# THE BATTLES

# LUKE SKYWALKER  VS. KYLO REN

Each warrior stands at the brink of understanding his full potential. Following his father's path to become a Jedi, young Luke Skywalker has just begun to learn the ways of the Force. Kylo Ren tries to live up to the menace of Darth Vader, but he is no Sith Lord.

## LUKE SKYWALKER

Once a simple farm boy from Tatooine, Luke Skywalker serves as a commander in the Rebel Alliance. His piloting skills and Force abilities allowed him to destroy the Empire's dreaded Death Star. Although he has learned much under Jedi Masters Obi-Wan Kenobi and Yoda, Luke is not a Jedi Knight yet.

## INFO

| | |
|---|---|
| Homeworld | Tatooine |
| Affiliation | Rebel Alliance/Jedi |
| Species | Human |
| Height/weight | 1.72 meters/73 kilograms |
| Weapons | Blaster, lightsaber (blue blade) |
| Special move | Flipping jump |

## STATS

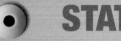

| Intelligence | Strength | Agility | Damage | Control | Courage |
|---|---|---|---|---|---|
| 7 | 8 | 7 | 6 | 8 | 10 |

# THE SHOWDOWN

Not recognizing this foe, Luke at first draws his blaster pistol. When Kylo ignites his lightsaber, the triple hiss of the central blade and two flanking vent blades make Luke realize his opponent is unusually dangerous. Kylo doesn't seek to capture Luke; he is out to destroy all Jedi. With Anakin Skywalker's lightsaber in hand, young Luke must do all he can to defend himself.

## KYLO REN

A dark warrior strong in the ways of the Force, Kylo Ren commands First Order missions with a temper as fiery as his unconventional lightsaber. He seeks to destroy any remaining Jedi who may pose a challenge to his rise to power.

## STATS

| Intelligence | Strength | Agility | Damage | Control | Courage |
|---|---|---|---|---|---|
| 7.5 | 8.5 | 7 | 7.5 | 8 | 8 |

## INFO

| | |
|---|---|
| Homeworld | Unknown |
| Affiliation | First Order/Knights of Ren |
| Species | Human |
| Height/weight | 1.89 meters/89 kilograms |
| Weapons | Custom crossblade lightsaber |
| Special move | Telekinetic halt |

Who wins?
See page 64.

5

# FINN VS. MAGNAGUARD DROID

Finn's flight from the ranks of the First Order has taken him to unexpected corners of the galaxy and brought him face-to-face with an outdated mechanical warrior from the Clone Wars. The precision-engineered MagnaGuard droids battled the Jedi in that long-ago conflict.

## FINN

A rigorously trained stormtrooper, Finn's conscience drives him to escape his past in the First Order and plunges him down a heroic but dangerous path. Finn scored high marks in simulated combat, but during his first combat mission, he had a profound change of heart.

### INFO

| | |
|---|---|
| Homeworld | Unknown |
| Affiliation | Resistance |
| Species | Human |
| Height/weight | 1.72 meters/73 kilograms |
| Weapons | Resistance BlasTech EL-16HFE blaster rifle |
| Special move | Sharpshooter stance |

### STATS

| Intelligence | Strength | Agility | Damage | Control | Courage |
|---|---|---|---|---|---|
| 5 | 7 | 5 | 6.5 | 7 | 7 |

# THE SHOWDOWN

The encounter begins at long range, making the MagnaGuard's lethal electrostaff useless. Instead, the droid fires its heavy blaster pistol. Finn returns fire, but the sturdily constructed MagnaGuard can take the hits. Closing in, it relentlessly plods toward Finn. Can Finn blast away his opponent before it gets close enough to use its electrostaff?

## MAGNAGUARD DROID

These IG-100 droids are trained in multiple forms of combat, both armed and unarmed. Of the entire droid army, these alone served as protectors to General Grievous.

## STATS

| Intelligence | Strength | Agility | Damage | Control | Courage |
|:---:|:---:|:---:|:---:|:---:|:---:|
| 5 | 9 | 6 | 7 | 6 | 6 |

## INFO

| | |
|---|---|
| **Homeworld** | Various |
| **Affiliation** | Separatist Alliance |
| **Manufacturer** | Holowan Mechanicals |
| **Droid Type** | IG-100 series bodyguard droid |
| **Height/weight** | 1.95 meters/123 kilograms |
| **Weapons** | Electrostaff, DT-57 annihilator blaster pistol |
| **Special move** | Staff twirl |

**Who wins?**
See page 64. **7**

The searing sunlight on desert planets makes it difficult for any living thing to survive. The inhabitants of Tatooine and Jakku have much in common. They are both tough and all too familiar with defending themselves against bandits, rivals, and intruders.

## REY

Rey is a resilient scavenger who has developed combat skills through a lifetime of dealing with the cutthroats on the harsh desert world of Jakku. Although she is of slight build, Rey is quick and agile, and capable of warding off threats with her metallic quarterstaff.

## STATS

| | |
|---|---|
| 6 | Intelligence |
| 6 | Strength |
| 6.5 | Agility |
| 4 | Damage |
| 7 | Control |
| 9 | Courage |

## INFO

| | |
|---|---|
| Homeworld | Jakku |
| Affiliation | Resistance |
| Species | Human |
| Height/weight | 1.7 meters/54 kilograms |
| Weapons | Staff |
| Special move | Pole vault double kick |

# THE SHOWDOWN

With a monstrous howl, the Tusken Raider raises his gaderffii stick over his head to intimidate Rey. She is not a skittish traveler, however. She waves her quarterstaff wide to keep the Tusken Raider at bay. The raider is undoubtedly stronger, but he cannot reach past Rey's guard to land a blow. Who will close the distance to strike first?

## TUSKEN RAIDER

Tusken Raiders, or Sand People, fiercely protect their territory. They can be easily startled, particularly in small numbers, but they often return to face their intruders in large groups.

## STATS

| Intelligence | Strength | Agility | Damage | Control | Courage |
|:---:|:---:|:---:|:---:|:---:|:---:|
| 5 | 8 | 4 | 6 | 6 | 6 |

## INFO

| | |
|---|---|
| Homeworld | Tatooine |
| Affiliation | Tusken |
| Species | Human |
| Height/weight | Average 1.9 meters/89 kilograms |
| Weapons | Gaderffii (gaffi) stick, sniper rifle |
| Special move | Gaderffii gash |

**Who wins?**
See page 64.

Poe's reputation as the best pilot in the Resistance has made him a target of the First Order. They issue a bounty on his head rather than risk their pilots. A skilled hunter from the past, Aurra Sing sees the hefty sum to be won, tracks Poe down, and plans her ground attack.

## POE DAMERON

An ace pilot, Poe Dameron is a leader in the Resistance's fight against the evil First Order. He soars into battle behind the controls of a modern X-wing fighter. But he isn't just a pilot; Poe is also a capable soldier.

### INFO

| | |
|---|---|
| Homeworld | Yavin 4 |
| Affiliation | Resistance |
| Species | Human |
| Height/weight | 1.72 meters/80 kilograms |
| Weapons | Resistance BlasTech EL-16 HFE blaster rifle, Glie-44 blaster pistol |
| Special move | Shoulder charge and tackle |

### STATS

| Intelligence | Strength | Agility | Damage | Control | Courage |
|---|---|---|---|---|---|
| 6 | 7 | 5 | 6.5 | 7 | 10 |

# THE SHOWDOWN

Aurra Sing sets her sniper rifle sight on Poe, but with his keen eyesight, Poe spots her before she can fire a shot. Turning on his hunter, Poe charges toward her, bobbing and weaving so that he's hard to hit. With her target too close to hit with her sniper rifle, Aurra Sing draws her twin blaster pistols and takes aim.

## AURRA SING

During the time of the Clone Wars, Aurra Sing was in her prime. Trained and raised by assassins, Sing doesn't rely on technology as much as other bounty hunters do. She doesn't even wear armor. If she finds herself disarmed, she can use her long, sharp fingers to cut and tear skin.

## STATS

| | | | | | |
|---|---|---|---|---|---|
| 6 | 6.5 | 7 | 6 | 7 | 6 |
| Intelligence | Strength | Agility | Damage | Control | Courage |

| | |
|---|---|
| **Homeworld** | Nar Shaddaa |
| **Affiliation** | Bounty hunter |
| **Species** | Human hybrid |
| **Height/weight** | 1.74 meters/56 kilograms |
| **Weapons** | Czerka Adventurer sniper rifle, pair of blaster pistols |
| **Special move** | Clawed swipe |

INFO

**Who wins?**
See page 64. 11

The squawking pet of the mighty Jabba the Hutt, Salacious Crumb is a pointy-clawed vandal who has been known to pick pockets and tear apart delicate technology. BB-8 is not one to enter a fight, but cornered, the round droid must defend himself from the cackling Crumb.

## BB-8

BB-8 is the spherical, loyal astromech droid of Resistance pilot Poe Dameron. This little droid is equipped to control the flight and power distribution systems of an X-wing starfighter. BB-8 has a variety of hidden tools, as well as data storage capacity.

### STATS

| | | | | | |
|---|---|---|---|---|---|
| 5.5 | 3 | 5 | 3 | 5 | 6 |
| Intelligence | Strength | Agility | Damage | Control | Courage |

### INFO

| | |
|---|---|
| Homeworld | Unknown |
| Affiliation | Resistance |
| Manufacturer | Unknown |
| Droid Type | Astromech droid |
| Height/weight | 0.67 meters/18 kilograms |
| Weapons | Retractable welding torch |
| Special move | Sudden direction change |

# THE SHOWDOWN

Salacious Crumb finds BB-8's rolling shape irresistibly fun—a finely constructed machine ready to be destroyed. Crumb leaps onto the droid, but the shrill-voiced monkey-lizard can't find a grip on his curved surface. This gives BB-8 time to deploy his hidden tool.

## SALACIOUS B. CRUMB

A Kowakian monkey-lizard with a haunting cackle, Salacious Crumb sat beside Jabba's throne, stealing bits of food and mimicking the Hutt, his courtiers, and visitors. The Hutt's noxious pet was the palace's unofficial court jester, tolerated because his antics amused Jabba.

## STATS

| | | | | | |
|---|---|---|---|---|---|
| 2.5 | 3.5 | 9 | 4 | 4 | 2.5 |
| Intelligence | Strength | Agility | Damage | Control | Courage |

## INFO

| | |
|---|---|
| Homeworld | Kowak |
| Affiliation | Criminal |
| Species | Kowakian monkey-lizard |
| Height/weight | 0.7 meters/9 kilograms |
| Weapons | Claws, beak |
| Special move | Tail-strangle |

**Who wins?**
See page 64.

It's a space battle across generations as a Resistance X-wing picks up an outdated TIE craft on its sensors. In its day, the TIE Advanced x1 was the cutting edge of Imperial starfighter technology. With Darth Vader at the controls, this ship incinerated many Rebel vessels, but can the classic hold its own against new starfighter technology?

## T-70 X-WING STARFIGHTER

This modern incarnation of the classic fighter design that defined the Rebel Alliance is a mainstay in the Resistance's starfighter corps. Improvements include refined engines, customizable weapons systems, and overall increased performance.

### INFO

| | |
|---|---|
| Manufacturer | Incom FreiTek |
| Affiliation | Resistance |
| Type | T-70 space superiority fighter |
| Length | 12.5 meters |
| Weapons | 4 laser cannons, 2 proton torpedo launchers |
| Top Speed | 1,300 kph (in atmosphere) |

### STATS

| Control | Hull | Maneuver | Speed | Firepower |
|---|---|---|---|---|
| 7 | 9 | 7.5 | 8 | 8.5 |

# THE SHOWDOWN

Both fighters streak forward, snapping off laser-cannon fire as they pass. Unlike the standard TIEs of the Old Empire era, the Advanced x1 has deflector shields, so it can slough off hits that would obliterate an unprotected ship. These defenses have limits, however, and the X-wing starfighter has increased speed and all-new weapons systems.

## TIE ADVANCED X1 STARFIGHTER

The distinctive experimental TIE fighter design was made famous by Darth Vader, who piloted the prototype into such historic engagements as the Battle of Yavin. It is an extremely maneuverable craft and more rugged and powerful than the standard TIE fighter.

## STATS

| Control | Hull | Maneuver | Speed | Firepower |
|---------|------|----------|-------|-----------|
| 7 | 6 | 8.5 | 7.5 | 5.5 |

### INFO

| | |
|---|---|
| Manufacturer | Sienar Fleet Systems |
| Affiliation | Galactic Empire |
| Type | Twin ion engine space superiority fighter |
| Length | 9.2 meters |
| Weapons | 2 laser cannons |
| Top Speed | 1,600 kph (in atmosphere) |

Who wins? See page 64.

# RATHTAR (VS.) DARTH VADER

Those unfortunate enough to have faced Darth Vader would not hesitate to describe the armored Sith Lord as a monster. But what if Vader had to face a *real* monster—a ravenous, mindless, and merciless rathtar?

## RATHTAR

Enormous tentacled beasts responsible for such disasters as the Trillia Massacre, rathtars are universally terrifying. Yet their intimidating presence, unique biology, and exotic rarity mean there's a demand for these creatures in the black market.

## STATS

| | | | | | |
|---|---|---|---|---|---|
| 2.5 | 20 | 8 | 10 | 4.5 | 4.5 |
| Intelligence | Strength | Agility | Damage | Control | Courage |

## INFO

| | |
|---|---|
| Homeworld | Unknown |
| Height/weight | 6.09 meters (with tentacles), 1.74 (body) /650 kilograms |
| Weapons | Tentacles, radial teeth |
| Special move | Tentacle grab |

# THE SHOWDOWN

Although investigating a derelict starship for information regarding a hidden rebel base, the Dark Lord mistakenly enters a trap. The starship's cargo hatch opens, and the deadly creature strikes, attempting to ensnare Vader in its sinewy tentacles. Vader ignites his lightsaber, but there are more vinelike graspers than his single blade can cut down at a time.

## DARTH VADER

Although terrifying, Darth Vader's dark armor hides the frail body of a broken man. He carries great anger at being trapped in a mechanical shell. This hatred powers him on his journey through the dark side of the Force.

## STATS

| 7 | 10 | 4 | 8 | 8 | 8 |
|---|----|---|---|---|---|
| Intelligence | Strength | Agility | Damage | Control | Courage |

| | |
|---|---|
| Homeworld | Tatooine |
| Affiliation | Sith, Galactic Empire |
| Species | Human |
| Height/weight | 2.02 meters/136 kilograms |
| Weapons | Lightsaber (red blade) |
| Special move | Lightsaber throw |

INFO

Who wins?
See page 64.

# REY'S SPEEDER  VS. LUKE'S LANDSPEEDER

Settlers living on harsh frontier worlds rely on sturdy technology to survive. The vehicles found on desert planets are scuffed and sandblasted by the tough environment. Some mechanics take pride in how beaten up their vehicles are, as long as they still function.

## REY'S SPEEDER

For quick transportation across the junk-strewn dunes of Jakku, Rey relies on her battered speeder. Cobbled together from desert salvage, Rey created a one-of-a-kind vehicle that is half speeder bike and half overpowered swoop.

### STATS

| | | | | |
|---|---|---|---|---|
| 3 | 2 | 7 | 5.5 | 1 |
| Control | Hull | Maneuver | Speed | Firepower |

### INFO

| | |
|---|---|
| Manufacturer | Custom special |
| Affiliation | Jakku scavenger |
| Type | Hybrid speeder/swoop |
| Length | 3.73 meters |
| Weapons | None |
| Top Speed | 450 kph |

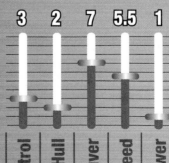

# THE SHOWDOWN

As neither vehicle has weapons, this is a battle of speed and durability. The two speeders take off across the desert sand. Although Rey's speeder is faster, it is quite difficult to control—something that may end up costing this imposing speeder the race.

## LUKE'S SPEEDER

As Luke grew up on Tatooine, he had few outlets from the daily chores on the moisture farm, but his reliable X-34 landspeeder provided him escape.

## STATS

| Control | Hull | Maneuver | Speed | Firepower |
|---------|------|----------|-------|-----------|
| 4 | 3 | 4 | 2.5 | 1 |

| | |
|---|---|
| **Manufacturer** | SoroSuub Corp. |
| **Affiliation** | Independent |
| **Type** | X-34 landspeeder |
| **Length** | 3.4 meters |
| **Weapons** | None |
| **Top Speed** | 250 kph |

INFO

**Who wins?**
See page 64.

# HAN SOLO VS. JANGO FETT

It's a head-to-head rematch! A previous edition pitted a young Han Solo against the legendary bounty hunter Jango Fett, in a brawl that (according to the experts) Fett would win. But with Han three decades older and wiser, can he best his opponent this time?

## HAN SOLO

After a lifetime of adventure, becoming a hero of the Rebel Alliance, and marrying a princess, the twists of fate have returned Han to the life of a law-bending smuggler. Older, wiser, and yet still daring and reckless, Solo is a talented pilot and crack shot.

### INFO

| | |
|---|---|
| Homeworld | Corellia |
| Affiliation | Smuggler |
| Species | Human |
| Height/weight | 1.8 meters/80 kilograms |
| Weapons | Modified BlasTech DL-44 heavy blaster pistol |
| Special move | Blind shot |

## STATS

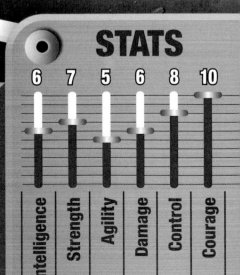

| Intelligence | Strength | Agility | Damage | Control | Courage |
|---|---|---|---|---|---|
| 6 | 7 | 5 | 6 | 8 | 10 |

# THE SHOWDOWN

Fett takes to the air with his jetpack, which keeps him just out of reach of the aging smuggler. Pressing his long-range advantage, Fett uses his arsenal to strike at Han from a distance.

## JANGO FETT

The deadliest bounty hunter of his time, Jango Fett wears a high-tech Mandalorian armor suit covered with weapons, including a built-in flamethrower, missile launcher, snare, and jetpack.

## STATS

| Intelligence | Strength | Agility | Damage | Control | Courage |
|---|---|---|---|---|---|
| 6 | 7 | 8 | 10 | 8 | 9 |

| | |
|---|---|
| Homeworld | Concord Dawn |
| Affiliation | Bounty hunter |
| Species | Human |
| Height/weight | 1.83 meters/79 kilograms |
| Weapons | Twin WESTAR-34 blaster pistols, rocket launcher, flamethrower, snare, rocket darts, climbing blades |
| Special move | Flamethrower attack |

INFO

**Who wins?**
See page 64.

21

# CHEWBACCA (VS.) GRUMMGAR

On a visit to his home planet of Kashyyyk, Chewbacca hears a commotion amid the trees. In one of the boughs, the brawny hunter Grummgar is tracking a wounded mylaya, a tree creature sacred to the Wookiees. Chewie lets loose a howling roar to draw Grummgar's attention.

## CHEWBACCA

Chewbacca is more a mechanic than a warrior, but he is fiercely strong—strong enough to pull an opponent's arms from their sockets. At more than 230 years old, Chewie is not even approaching middle age for the long-lived Wookiee species.

## STATS

| | 6 | 10 | 4 | 8 | 6 | 7 |
|---|---|---|---|---|---|---|
| | Intelligence | Strength | Agility | Damage | Control | Courage |

## INFO

| | |
|---|---|
| Homeworld | Kashyyyk |
| Affiliation | Smuggler |
| Species | Wookiee |
| Height/weight | 2.28 meters/115 kilograms |
| Weapons | Bowcaster |
| Special move | Arm-ripper pull |

# THE SHOWDOWN

The echoing Wookiee roar causes Grummgar to lose his focus and put down his rifle. The sacred creature leaps away to safety. Chewbacca accomplished what he set out to do, but the Grummgar has been deprived of his quarry. Although a Wookiee pelt is not as rare or treasured, it will still command a price on the black market. The hunter has his next target: Chewbacca!

## GRUMMGAR

A big game hunter with a huge build and an ego to match, obsessed with trophies. The unsavory Dowutin often bends the law, poaching rare and endangered creatures in the wilds of distant worlds.

## STATS

| Intelligence | Strength | Agility | Damage | Control | Courage |
|---|---|---|---|---|---|
| 5.5 | 11 | 4.5 | 7 | 6.5 | 6 |

| | |
|---|---|
| Homeworld | Unknown |
| Affiliation | Criminal |
| Species | Dowutin |
| Height/weight | 2.7 meters/156 kilograms |
| Weapons | Custom hunting rifle, grenades |
| Special move | Horned chin-butt |

Who wins?
See page 64.

All across the galaxy lay scattered wreckage of the war between the Rebel Alliance and the Galactic Empire. Functional technology can be refurbished and put back into action, as reports of still-active T-65 X-wings in frontier sectors indicate.

## SPECIAL FORCES TIE FIGHTER

The elite First Order pilots fly specialized craft, such as the two-seater TIE/sf—a variant with enhanced weapon and sensor systems. Unlike most TIE fighters, the Special Forces version includes a hyperdrive. The tail gunner operates a swivel cannon that can fire forward and backward.

## STATS

| Control | Hull | Maneuver | Speed | Firepower |
|---------|------|----------|-------|-----------|
| 6.5 | 9 | 8 | 7 | 9 |

### INFO

| | |
|---|---|
| **Manufacturer** | Sienar-Jaemus Fleet Systems |
| **Affiliation** | First Order |
| **Type** | TIE/sf space superiority fighter |
| **Length** | 6.69 meters long |
| **Weapons** | Two laser cannons, dual heavy laser turret, concussion missiles, mag-pulse warhead launcher |
| **Top Speed** | 1,150 kph (in atmosphere) |

# THE SHOWDOWN

One of these antiquated X-wings crosses an invisible border into First Order space. A special forces TIE fighter is scrambled to intercept. The X-wing s-foils split into attack position. It is a formidable fighter, and its deflector shields and armor can withstand volleys of incoming fire—but can it outmaneuver the newer, more sophisticated ship?

## T-65 X-WING FIGHTER

The Incom T-65 X-wing fighter made famous by the Rebel Alliance is a dependable general-purpose starfighter with four laser cannons on its wings and two proton torpedo launchers on its hull. An astromech droid assists with in-flight repairs.

## STATS

| 6 | 8 | 7 | 7 | 8 |
|---|---|---|---|---|
| Control | Hull | Maneuver | Speed | Firepower |

| INFO | |
|---|---|
| Manufacturer | Incom Corp. |
| Affiliation | Rebel Alliance |
| Type | T-65 space superiority fighter |
| Length | 12.5 meters long |
| Weapons | 4 laser cannons, 2 proton torpedo launchers |
| Top Speed | 1,050 kph (in atmosphere) |

**Who wins?**
See page 64.

# TEEDO (VS.) JAWA

A scuffle between these combatants can be over only one thing: a droid. These desert scavengers are both drawn to unguarded and wandering mechanicals, stalking the dunes and crags for robotic prey.

## TEEDO

Teedos are small, brutish scavengers that roam the Jakku wilderness, often riding atop cyborg luggabeasts. Teedos have a peculiar sense of individual identity. The name Teedo identifies both the species and each member within it.

## STATS

| Intelligence | Strength | Agility | Damage | Control | Courage |
|---|---|---|---|---|---|
| 6 | 4.5 | 6 | 3.5 | 4 | 7 |

## INFO

| | |
|---|---|
| Homeworld | Jakku |
| Affiliation | None |
| Height/weight | Average 1.26 meters/28 kilograms |
| Weapons | Ionization spear |
| Special move | Spear jab |

# THE SHOWDOWN

As both scavengers eye the same quarry, they draw their weapons. However, these devices are designed to cripple droid targets. The Jawa's ionization blaster grants the advantage of range, but the Teedo has foolhardy courage, which will help him get close enough to jab the Jawa with his ionization spear.

## JAWA

Jawas are small scavengers and are highly resistant to disease and extreme heat. When traveling outside the safety of their massive sandcrawlers, they are skittish, traveling only in groups to ambush their mechanical prey.

## STATS

| 5 | 4 | 7 | 4 | 4 | 2 |
|---|---|---|---|---|---|
| Intelligence | Strength | Agility | Damage | Control | Courage |

| | |
|---|---|
| Homeworld | Tatooine |
| Affiliation | None |
| Height/weight | Average 0.97 meter/30 kilograms |
| Weapons | Ionization blaster |
| Special move | Nasty stench |

INFO

Who wins?
See page 64.

27

When the New Republic came to power, it instituted a disarmament program with the aim of preventing future galactic wars. Enormous warships such as the kind developed by the Empire became exceedingly rare. Little did the New Republic suspect that the First Order was busily developing even larger warships on the far side of the galaxy.

## FIRST ORDER STAR DESTROYER

An enormous symbol of power in addition to being an incredibly complex warship, the *Resurgent-*class Star Destroyer bears the dagger-shaped profile of old Imperial ships. These ships are spacebound cities, with loyal First Order soldiers training, working, and living their whole lives on board.

## STATS

| | | | | |
|---|---|---|---|---|
| 8 | 250 | 1 | 4.5 | 40 |
| Control | Hull | Maneuver | Speed | Firepower |

### INFO

| | |
|---|---|
| Manufacturer | Kuat-Entralla Engineering |
| Affiliation | First Order |
| Type | *Resurgent*-class Star Destroyer |
| Length | 2,915 meters long |
| Weapons | More than 3,000 turbolasers, missile turrets, and ion cannons |
| Top Speed | 775 kph (in atmosphere) |

# THE SHOWDOWN

The emergence of the *Resurgent*-class Star Destroyer from hyperspace comes as a complete shock to the crew of the MC80 because vessels this big are outlawed in New Republic space! The First Order gunners care little for interstellar law, and they begin targeting the weapons and engine systems of the smaller craft.

## MON CALAMARI STAR CRUISER

The backbone of the original Rebel Alliance fleet, the distinctive MC80 star cruiser is a product of the Mon Calamari, the soulful aquatic species. After the Alliance became the New Republic, most of the interstellar fleet was dismantled, though a few of the old ships still protect Mon Cala and other Republic worlds.

## STATS

| | | | | |
|---|---|---|---|---|
| 8.5 | 125 | 1 | 5 | 20 |
| Control | Hull | Maneuver | Speed | Firepower |

| | |
|---|---|
| **Manufacturer** | Mon Calamari shipyards |
| **Affiliation** | Rebel Alliance |
| **Type** | MC80 star cruiser |
| **Length** | 1,200 meters |
| **Weapons** | 48 turbolaser batteries, 20 ion cannon batteries, 6 tractor beam projectors |
| **Top Speed** | 975 kph (in atmosphere) |

INFO

Who wins?
See page 64.

29

# FIRST ORDER STORMTROOPER  CLONE TROOPER

The face of galactic warfare has changed in the generations between the Clone Wars and the rise of the First Order. Yet the look of the black-and-white armor first worn by the clone troopers of the Republic has not. Both armies expected their soldiers to conform but through very different means.

## FIRST ORDER STORMTROOPER

First Order stormtroopers are trained from birth through a rigorous program of simulations and physical drills. These soldiers are not given individual names and are instead referred to only by numbers. They are far more effective than the stormtroopers of the Old Empire.

## STATS

| Intelligence | Strength | Agility | Damage | Control | Courage |
| --- | --- | --- | --- | --- | --- |
| 5 | 7 | 5 | 7 | 7 | 8 |

### INFO

| | |
| --- | --- |
| Homeworld | Various |
| Affiliation | First Order |
| Species | Human |
| Height/weight | Average 1.83 meters/80 kilograms |
| Weapons | Sonn-Blas F-11D blaster rifle, Sonn-Blas SE-44C blaster pistol |
| Special move | Targeted strike |

# THE SHOWDOWN

The clone trooper is highly trained and ready to defend himself, but as the forerunner to the stormtrooper he may be at a disadvantage. The stormtrooper, having studied a wide variety of combat scenarios, may already know what the clone trooper plans to do.

## CLONE TROOPER

Clone troopers were created from Jango Fett, the galaxy's most skilled bounty hunter during the twilight of the Galactic Republic. Although they are physically identical, these highly trained soldiers have rich, individual personalities, especially after encouragement by and interaction with their Jedi generals.

## STATS

| | | | | | |
|---|---|---|---|---|---|
| 5 | 7 | 5 | 6 | 7 | 8 |
| Intelligence | Strength | Agility | Damage | Control | Courage |

| | |
|---|---|
| Homeworld | Kamino |
| Affiliation | Galactic Republic |
| Species | Human |
| Height/weight | 1.83 meters/80 kilograms |
| Weapons | DC-15S blaster rifle, DC-15A blaster rifle |
| Special move | Martial arts |

INFO

**Who wins?**
See page 64.

# HAPPABORE  VS. REEK

It's getting tense around the feeding trough as a surly reek and happabore are vying for the last of the slop. The reek is more innately territorial than the domesticated happabore, but the happabore is not exactly a pushover.

## HAPPABORE

Found on multiple worlds as a result of ancient colonization efforts, the happabore is a strong, hardy creature with tough skin and remarkable obedience. They are used as pack and riding animals by all manner of beings.

## STATS

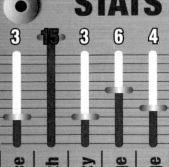

| Intelligence | Strength | Agility | Damage | Courage |
|:---:|:---:|:---:|:---:|:---:|
| 3 | 15 | 3 | 6 | 4 |

## INFO

| | |
|---|---|
| Homeworld | Various |
| Height/weight | Average 5.9 meters long/2,500 kilograms |
| Weapons | Tusks |
| Special move | Trample |

# THE SHOWDOWN

The short-tempered reek stamps the ground with its leathery foot and snorts jets of hot air. It lowers its head for a charge. The happabore hunkers down on its four stout legs. For the reek, it's like ramming a stone wall; the massive happabore barely budges. The air echoes with the irritated groans and grunts of angered titans.

## REEK

Despite their massive horns and tough skin, reeks are not naturally dangerous. The ones used for arena fighting, however, are often abused and starved until they are highly aggressive.

## STATS

| 2 | 15 | 4 | 9 | 5 |
|---|----|---|---|---|
| Intelligence | Strength | Agility | Damage | Courage |

| | |
|---|---|
| Homeworld | Codian Moon |
| Height/weight | Average 2.24 meters/1,100 kilograms |
| Weapons | Teeth, horns |
| Special move | Bite |

INFO

**Who wins?**
See page 64.

33

Each ship is a reflection of the pilot: the *Falcon*'s ramshackle appearance mirrors Captain Han Solo's checkered past, while Kylo Ren's shuttle is tall, dark, and unmistakably deadly.

## MILLENNIUM FALCON

One of the most coveted ships in the galaxy, the *Falcon* is very fast, and its shields and firepower are downright illegal. The freighter has two turret-mounted quad laser cannons and carries concussion missiles.

### INFO

| Manufacturer | Corellian Engineering Corp. |
|---|---|
| Affiliation | Smuggler |
| Type | Modified YT-1300 light freighter |
| Size | 34.75 meters long |
| Weapons | 2 quad laser cannons, 2 concussion missile tubes, 1 antipersonnel blaster |
| Top Speed | 1,050 kph (in atmosphere) |

### STATS

| Control | Hull | Maneuver | Speed | Firepower |
|---|---|---|---|---|
| 5 | 6 | 7 | 7.5 | 6 |

# THE SHOWDOWN

The shuttle extends its batlike wings, spreading its deflector shield coverage into an invisible web surrounding the craft. The *Falcon*'s shields cut in and out as a result of a new glitch introduced during its last overhaul, but its engines are operating at peak capacity. Can it outrun the shuttle while also firing in its rear arc to take out its pursuer?

## KYLO REN'S SHUTTLE

The *Upsilon*-class shuttle's enormous stabilizer wings serve as deflector shield projection as well as sensor surfaces, providing the ship with impressive targeting and resistance to incoming fire.

## STATS

| | | | | |
|---|---|---|---|---|
| 6 | 7 | 6.5 | 7 | 4 |
| Control | Hull | Maneuver | Speed | Firepower |

| | |
|---|---|
| **Manufacturer** | Sienar-Jaemus Fleet Systems |
| **Affiliation** | First Order |
| **Type** | *Upsilon*-class shuttle |
| **Size** | 37.2 meters (wings extended) |
| **Weapons** | 2 twin laser cannons |
| **Top Speed** | 950 kph (in atmosphere) |

INFO

**Who wins?**
See page 64.

# CAPTAIN PHASMA  VS. BOBA FETT

It's an armored brawl as the faceless Fett and fearless Phasma do battle. The towering Phasma is a commanding presence in her gleaming armor, but the battle-pitted Mandalorian suit that Fett wears has proven its worth time and again.

## CAPTAIN PHASMA

Clad in distinctive brushed chromium armor, Captain Phasma commands the First Order's legion of troops. Despite her rank, she prefers frontline service, entering into combat beside her enlisted soldiers.

### INFO

| | |
|---|---|
| Homeworld | Unknown |
| Affiliation | First Order |
| Species | Human |
| Height/weight | 1.93 meters/76 kilograms |
| Weapons | Chrome-finished Sonn-Blas F-11D blaster rifle, crush-gauntlets |
| Special move | Martial arts |

### STATS

| Intelligence | Strength | Agility | Damage | Control | Courage |
|---|---|---|---|---|---|
| 7 | 8 | 7 | 6 | 8.5 | 10 |

# THE SHOWDOWN

Phasma has studied the clone trooper ranks that share Boba Fett's DNA. She knows what such soldiers are capable of, so she keeps a careful eye on Fett. As Boba Fett unleashes his flamethrower, Phasma easily dodges the attack. A second blast catches Phasma, but it appears to have little effect on the captain's metal-clad form.

## BOBA FETT

Boba Fett was the perfect genetic duplicate of his "father," Jango Fett. He wears a battered version of Jango's armored battle suit, a design from the ancient Mandalorian culture, but Fett is no traditionalist; he wears the armor for its lethal functionality.

## STATS

| Intelligence | Strength | Agility | Damage | Control | Courage |
|---|---|---|---|---|---|
| 7 | 8 | 7 | 7 | 9 | 9 |

INFO

| | |
|---|---|
| Homeworld | Kamino |
| Affiliation | Bounty hunter |
| Species | Human |
| Height/weight | 1.83 meters/78 kilograms |
| Weapons | EE-3 blaster rifle, heavy carbine, flamethrower, rocket launcher, rocket darts, snare |
| Special move | Flamethrower attack |

**Who wins?**
See page 64.

# TIE/FO FIGHTER (VS.) JEDI STARFIGHTER

To pave the way for galactic dominance, the First Order sought to eradicate any remnants of the Jedi remaining since the fall of the Empire. But a blast from the Jedi past streaks across the sensor scopes of a First Order TIE fighter. Enter a tiny, nimble Jedi starfighter, ready for action!

## TIE/FO STARFIGHTER

Advances in technology and changes in military needs have made the new-generation TIE fighter far less disposable than the vessels of the Old Empire. These standard TIEs even come equipped with rudimentary deflector shields and improved pilot survival equipment.

**INFO**

| | |
|---|---|
| Manufacturer | Sienar-Jaemus Fleet Systems |
| Affiliation | First Order |
| Type | TIE/FO fighter |
| Size | 6.69 meters long |
| Weapons | 2 laser cannons |
| Top Speed | 1,260 kph (in atmosphere) |

## STATS

| Control | Hull | Maneuver | Speed | Firepower |
|---|---|---|---|---|
| 6.5 | 6 | 7 | 8 | 6 |

38

The small arrowhead-shaped Jedi fighter darts about, making it difficult for the TIE fighter's sensors to peg it into a targeting grid. The TIE pilot fires, attempting to bracket the Jedi fighter and force it to expend its limited fuel supply. The vessels are evenly matched for speed, but the Jedi fighter has a slightly tighter turn radius. The fighters chase each other in an increasingly small spiral.

## JEDI STARFIGHTER

The tiny Delta-7 Jedi starfighter is extremely compact and carries two laser cannons as well as two torpedo launchers. Like other small vessels of its era, it lacks a hyperdrive and instead relies upon a dockable hyperspace transport ring for lightspeed travel.

## STATS

| Control | Hull | Maneuver | Speed | Firepower |
|---------|------|----------|-------|-----------|
| 7 | 6 | 8 | 8 | 6.5 |

**INFO**

| | |
|---|---|
| **Manufacturer** | Kuat Systems Engineering |
| **Affiliation** | Jedi |
| **Type** | Delta-7 *Aethersprite*-class interceptor |
| **Size** | 8 meters long |
| **Weapons** | 2 laser cannons, 2 torpedo launchers |
| **Top Speed** | 1,260 kph (in atmosphere) |

**Who wins?**
See page 64.

# SNAP WEXLEY (VS.) TIE FIGHTER PILOT

Starfighter pilots deeply identify with their starships, thinking of the vessels as an extension of their bodies. It's rare that two pilots would enter into combat without their beloved ships, but it's been known to happen.

## SNAP WEXLEY

An ace Resistance X-wing pilot, Snap Wexley serves as a recon pilot with keen eyes to spot trouble, and expert flying skills to evade it. He follows Poe Dameron's command as part of Blue Squadron.

### STATS

| | |
|---|---|
| Intelligence | 6.5 |
| Strength | 6.5 |
| Agility | 4 |
| Damage | 5 |
| Control | 7.5 |
| Courage | 8 |

### INFO

| | |
|---|---|
| Homeworld | Akiva |
| Affiliation | Resistance |
| Species | Human |
| Height/weight | 1.88 meters tall/110 kilograms |
| Weapons | Glie-44 blaster pistol |
| Special move | Akivan bare-knuckle boxing |

# THE SHOWDOWN

Both Snap Wexley and the TIE fighter pilot are trained in hand-to-hand combat, although with very different disciplines. The TIE pilot's Imperial Academy training includes formal fighting techniques. Snap, on the other hand, learned self-defense in the streets of Akiva, his embattled homeworld.

## TIE FIGHTER PILOT

Replacing the clone pilots of the Galactic Republic, the fighter jocks of the Imperial Starfleet were the product of rigorous academy training. Before the rise of the Rebel Alliance starfighter forces, TIE pilots rarely encountered comparable resistance—so they tend to be insufferably cocky.

## STATS

| | | | | | |
|---|---|---|---|---|---|
| 6 | 6 | 5 | 5 | 7 | 7 |
| Intelligence | Strength | Agility | Damage | Control | Courage |

| | |
|---|---|
| Homeworld | Various |
| Affiliation | Galactic Empire |
| Species | Human |
| Height/weight | Average 1.83 meters/80 kilograms |
| Weapons | E-11 blaster rifle |
| Special move | Academy martial arts |

INFO

**Who wins?** See page 64.

# CONSTABLE ZUVIO  VS. GUAVIAN SECURITY SOLDIER

Crime is on the rise as the galactic powers march toward war. Local law enforcement can't rely on extra help to keep order, especially on frontier worlds such as Jakku. Constable Zuvio does what he can to prevent violence at Niima Outpost, but a fearsome Guavian Death Gang hitman is looking to cause trouble.

## CONSTABLE ZUVIO

The leader of a local militia tasked to keep crime from ruining business in the trading stalls of Niima Outpost, Zuvio has a sense of justice that seems too big for such a small town. The ever-vigilant Zuvio cannot be bribed.

## INFO

| | |
|---|---|
| **Homeworld** | Phatrong |
| **Affiliation** | Jakku Constabulary |
| **Species** | Kyuzo |
| **Height/weight** | 1.6 meters/70 kilograms |
| **Weapons** | Salvaged metal vibro-halberd, concealed blaster pistol, armored shield/Kyuzo war hat |
| **Special move** | Daring disc hat-throw |

## STATS

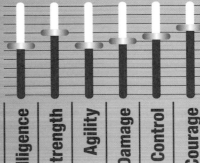

| Intelligence | Strength | Agility | Damage | Control | Courage |
|---|---|---|---|---|---|
| 5.5 | 7 | 5.5 | 6 | 6.5 | 7.5 |

# THE SHOWDOWN

Zuvio barks out orders for the Guavian soldier to stand down. When he gets no response, Zuvio pulls out a blaster pistol and fires into the air to draw the security soldier's attention. The Guavian is not intimidated, however. He fires a return shot with his percussive cannon. Zuvio thrusts his armored helmet in the path of the blast to deflect it. The impact hurls him backward. As Zuvio struggles to his feet, the Guavian charges.

## GUAVIAN SECURITY SOLDIERS

The red-armored foot soldiers of the notorious Guavian Death Gang are faceless enforcers who undergo cybernetic modification to make them more effective warriors. A mechanical reservoir acts as a second, artificial heart, and pumps them full of secret chemicals to enhance their speed and aggressiveness.

## STATS

| Intelligence | Strength | Agility | Damage | Control | Courage |
| --- | --- | --- | --- | --- | --- |
| 5 | 7.5 | 5 | 7.5 | 6 | 10 |

## INFO

| | |
| --- | --- |
| Homeworld | Various |
| Affiliation | Guavian Death Gang |
| Species | Various humanoids |
| Height/weight | 1.6 meters/70 kilograms |
| Weapons | Percussive cannon |
| Special move | Fearless charge |

**Who wins?**
See page 64.

If the Jedi Order existed in these troubled days of the New Republic, they would have worked tirelessly to stop criminal gangs such as the notorious Kanjiklub. But since the Jedi have faded into history, a marauder like Tasu Leech need not worry about anyone stopping his pirating ways. Imagine his surprise when he encounters Jedi Aayla Secura.

## TASU LEECH

The current leader of the Kanjiklub gang, Tasu is an unruly street fighter who holds on to his command position by not showing any signs of weakness. Tasu grew up on the frontiers of the galaxy, clawing his way to the top. He refuses to speak Basic, considering it a weak tongue of an unworthy people.

### INFO

| | |
|---|---|
| Homeworld | Nar Kanji |
| Affiliation | Kanjiklub |
| Species | Human |
| Height/weight | 1.57 meters/62 kilograms |
| Weapons | Huttsplitter overpower blaster rifle with vibro-spike bayonet, concealed vibroblade |
| Special move | Unarmed nerve cluster punch |

## STATS

| Intelligence | Strength | Agility | Damage | Control | Courage |
|---|---|---|---|---|---|
| 6 | 7.5 | 8.5 | 6 | 7 | 8 |

# THE SHOWDOWN

Tasu surprises Aayla by not showing any hesitation when confronted by a Jedi Knight. The impulsive pirate draws his oversized blaster and fires. Aayla deflects the shot with her lightsaber, but the oversized bolt hammers her blade, making it hard to deflect accurately. Tasu grins ferociously, realizing this fight may be won in close quarters, an arena in which he excels.

## AAYLA SECURA

A young Jedi Knight during the Clone Wars, Aayla rose to the challenge of becoming a general in the galactic conflict, maturing quickly during such dire times. An acrobatic Twi'lek, she is an expert hand-to-hand combatant. A kick from her strong legs can end a duel as quickly as a slash from her lightsaber.

## STATS

| | | | | | |
|---|---|---|---|---|---|
| 7 | 7.5 | 7.5 | 9 | 8 | 10 |
| Intelligence | Strength | Agility | Damage | Control | Courage |

### INFO

| | |
|---|---|
| Homeworld | Ryloth |
| Affiliation | Jedi Order |
| Species | Twi'lek |
| Height/weight | 1.72 meters/55 kilograms |
| Weapons | Lightsaber (blue blade) |
| Special move | Nexu-stance evasive roll |

**Who wins?**
See page 64.

# BAZINE NETAL (VS.) ZAM WESELL

Looks can be deceiving and falling for that deception can be deadly. In the assassin trade, fatales like Bazine Netal and Zam Wesell mask their dangerous intent with attractive forms, but none of their disguises will work when they face off against each other.

## BAZINE NETAL

A mysterious beauty who can disappear in crowds through skilled misdirection and lithe grace, Bazine Netal is willing to spy for the highest bidder. During the rise of the First Order, she was well compensated to keep an eye out for Resistance activity.

## STATS

| Intelligence | Strength | Agility | Damage | Control | Courage |
| --- | --- | --- | --- | --- | --- |
| 7 | 5.5 | 6.5 | 6 | 7 | 7 |

### INFO

| | |
| --- | --- |
| Homeworld | Unknown |
| Affiliation | First Order |
| Species | Human |
| Height/weight | 1.7 meters/55 kilograms |
| Weapons | Poison, custom hold-out blaster |
| Special move | Acrobatic disarm |

# THE SHOWDOWN

Zam's changeling abilities give her a physiological advantage, but adopting new forms requires concentration. Bazine is determined to keep Zam distracted. As the two clash, Zam's gear proves more dangerous, but Bazine is used to traveling fast and light.

## ZAM WESELL

A bounty hunter during the twilight of the Galactic Republic, Zam was comfortable with rifles, explosives and poisons. As a Clawdite, she can change shape to impersonate any humanoid close to her size. She avoids wearing heavy armor because it interferes with her shape-shifting abilities.

## STATS

| Intelligence | Strength | Agility | Damage | Control | Courage |
|:---:|:---:|:---:|:---:|:---:|:---:|
| 5 | 6 | 6 | 7 | 6 | 6 |

| | |
|---|---|
| **Homeworld** | Zolan |
| **Affiliation** | Bounty hunter |
| **Species** | Clawdite |
| **Height/weight** | 1.68 meters/55 kilograms |
| **Weapons** | KiSteer 1284 sniper rifle, KYD-21 blaster pistol, cylinder of deadly kouhuns |
| **Special move** | Changeling choke hold |

INFO

**Who wins?**
See page 64.

47

# FIRST ORDER SNOWTROOPER  VS. REBEL COMMANDO

During the Galactic Civil War, the Rebel Alliance military had to be the best out of necessity, as they were greatly outnumbered by the Imperial forces. Now, thirty years later, as the First Order rises in power, a new generation of rebels has learned from the previous victories and stepped up their training programs to make their soldiers more effective.

## FIRST ORDER SNOWTROOPER

Specialist soldiers in the First Order stormtrooper ranks, the cold assault soldiers, or "snowtroopers," were stationed throughout the massive Starkiller Base operation and on frigid worlds conquered in the name of the Supreme Leader.

### INFO

| | |
|---|---|
| **Homeworld** | Various |
| **Affiliation** | First Order |
| **Species** | Human |
| **Height/weight** | Average 1.8 meters/80 kilograms |
| **Weapons** | Sonn-Blas F-11D blaster rifle |
| **Special move** | Targeted strike |

## STATS

| Intelligence | Strength | Agility | Damage | Control | Courage |
|---|---|---|---|---|---|
| 5 | 7.5 | 5 | 6.5 | 7 | 7 |

# THE SHOWDOWN

In a snow-covered forest, both troopers rush forward, setting aside defense for a quick-strike victory. Short, controlled rifle bursts cover each soldier's advance as they duck from tree to rock to tree, closing the distance between them. Each combatant stands with his back to a tree, ready to jump out and fire at their enemy.

## REBEL COMMANDO

Rebel special forces—or SpecForces—hail from a wide variety of planets, many of them from Outer Rim Worlds subjugated by the Empire. Although they do not benefit from Academy training like their Imperial foes, Rebel commandos are trained by former Imperials.

## STATS

| Intelligence | Strength | Agility | Damage | Control | Courage |
|---|---|---|---|---|---|
| 5 | 6 | 5 | 6.5 | 6.5 | 8.5 |

| | |
|---|---|
| Homeworld | Various |
| Affiliation | Rebel Alliance |
| Species | Various, including human |
| Height/weight | Average 1.8 meters/80 kilograms |
| Weapons | BlasTech A280 blaster rifle, survival knife, thermal detonator |
| Special move | Rifle-butt swing |

INFO

**Who wins?**
See page 64.

In this time-twisting battle, a decorated Imperial general faces off against the seasoned leader of the Resistance. General Veers is a sterling example of an Imperial officer, and although Leia has not faced frontline combat in years, she is determined to rid the galaxy of oppression.

## GENERAL LEIA ORGANA

Leia's adamant suspicions regarding the intentions and actions of the First Order caused a rift between her and the New Republic Senate. Angered by the government's refusal to act, she set out to create her own defense force—the Resistance.

## STATS

| Intelligence | Strength | Agility | Damage | Control | Courage |
| --- | --- | --- | --- | --- | --- |
| 9.5 | 6 | 4 | 5 | 7 | 10 |

### INFO

| | |
| --- | --- |
| Homeworld | Alderaan |
| Affiliation | Resistance |
| Species | Human |
| Height/weight | 1.5 meters/51 kilograms |
| Weapons | Glie-44 blaster pistol |
| Special move | Fast draw |

# THE SHOWDOWN

Veers dons his armored chest plate and helmet, while Leia makes do with just her slim sidearm. In the command center of the hidden D'Qar base, Veers shouts for Leia to surrender, punctuating his command with blaster fire. Leia stays safe behind a communications console, putting her home-turf advantage to work. Confident that he has intimidated his enemy, Veers steps deeper into the control room.

## GENERAL VEERS

An effective and decorated Imperial officer, General Veers earned the respect of his peers through an impressive record of ground combat. Veers led the critical strike against the Alliance base on Hoth, commanding the squadron of AT-AT walkers that thundered across the icy plains to victory.

## STATS

| Intelligence | Strength | Agility | Damage | Control | Courage |
|---|---|---|---|---|---|
| 7 | 6.5 | 5 | 6 | 5 | 9 |

**INFO**

| | |
|---|---|
| Homeworld | Unknown |
| Affiliation | Galactic Empire |
| Species | Human |
| Height/weight | 1.93 meters/82 kilograms |
| Weapons | E-11 blaster rifle |
| Special move | Intimidation |

**Who wins?**
See page 64.

# CAPTAIN SIDON ITHANO  VS. GENERAL GRIEVOUS

General Grievous is a proud Kaleesh warrior; he still wears his traditional war mask even when so little of his original form remains. If he were to learn an insolent pirate wore a similar mask simply for effect, the ill-tempered cyborg would not let it stand.

## CAPTAIN SIDON ITHANO

The era of lawlessness that followed the Galactic Civil War led to the rise of this pirate. Captain Ithano is the subject of many an exaggerated cantina tale. He encourages the tales of the Red Raider, the Crimson Corsair, and the Blood Buccaneer. Ithano hopes his reputation will do all the hard work for him.

### INFO

| | |
|---|---|
| Homeworld | Unknown |
| Affiliation | Criminal |
| Species | Delphidian |
| Height/weight | 1.83/80 kilograms |
| Weapons | Captured Kanjiklub heavy bore blaster rifle |
| Special move | Disarming kick |

### STATS

| Intelligence | Strength | Agility | Damage | Control | Courage |
|---|---|---|---|---|---|
| 7.5 | 9 | 9 | 8 | 7 | 5 |

# THE SHOWDOWN

Grievous loudly accuses Ithano of being a thief. The red-clad brigand scoffs. A "thief" is pretty much the definition of a pirate. This only enrages Grievous further. The cyborg general extracts his lightsabers from the pockets in his cape. Ithano has never seen such weapons in action before, but he looks forward to adding another tale to the legend of the Red Raider.

## GENERAL GRIEVOUS

Beneath the bonelike armor of Grievous beats the heart of an evil warlord. He lacks the natural Force talents of a Jedi. Instead, he relies on his cunning and mechanical exoskeleton to transform himself into a whirling, lightsaber-wielding warrior.

## STATS

| Intelligence | Strength | Agility | Damage | Control | Courage |
|---|---|---|---|---|---|
| 6 | 8 | 6 | 7.5 | 7 | 6 |

| | |
|---|---|
| Homeworld | Kalee |
| Affiliation | Separatist Alliance |
| Species | Kaleesh |
| Height/weight | 2.02 meters/159 kilograms |
| Weapons | Captured Jedi lightsabers, electrostaff, DT-57 "Annihilator" blaster pistol |
| Special move | Four-arm whirlwind with lightsabers |

INFO

**Who wins?** See page 64.

# FIRST ORDER SNOWSPEEDER  VS. AAT ASSAULT TANK

Combat vehicles from across eras square off! The swift "flying jeep" of a utility vehicle from the First Order attempts to destroy the heavily armored and armed tank that's more than sixty years old.

## FIRST ORDER SNOWSPEEDER

These fast, versatile utility vehicles are essentially a pair of seats on a cargo flatbed converted into a weapons platform. They are deployed by the First Order for transport and defense in subzero climates.

| INFO | |
|---|---|
| Manufacturer | Aratech-Jaemus Corporation |
| Affiliation | First Order |
| Type | Infantry light utility vehicle |
| Size | 5.26 meters long |
| Weapons | 1 FWMB-10 repeating blaster |
| Top Speed | 250 kph |

## STATS

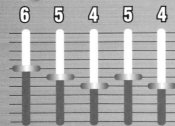

| Control | Hull | Maneuver | Speed | Firepower |
|---|---|---|---|---|
| 6 | 5 | 4 | 5 | 4 |

# THE SHOWDOWN

The fast and agile snowspeeder quickly closes the distance between the vehicles, making the AAT's most powerful cannon ineffective at such tight range. The AAT still has plenty of other weapons, however, including antipersonnel blasters.

## AAT TANK

As the main armored combat vehicle of the Trade Federation and Separatist Alliance droid army, the AAT assault tank is a weapons-laden, thickly armored repulsorcraft operated by a crew of battle droids.

## STATS

| | | | | |
|---|---|---|---|---|
| 5 | 8 | 4 | 4 | 5 |
| Control | Hull | Maneuver | Speed | Firepower |

| | |
|---|---|
| **Manufacturer** | Baktoid Armor Corp. |
| **Affiliation** | Trade Federation |
| **Type** | Armored assault tank |
| **Size** | 9.19 meters long |
| **Weapons** | Primary turret laser cannon, twin lateral range-finding laser cannons, twin lateral antipersonnel blasters, 6 energy-shell projectile launchers |
| **Top Speed** | 55 kph |

INFO

**Who wins?**
See page 64.

# GENERAL HUX VS. GENERAL MADINE

It's rare for military commanders to engage in single combat. The constantly outnumbered Rebel Alliance officers accompanied soldiers onto the battlefield at times, but it is a rarer event in the First Order. General Hux and General Madine both take pride in their ability to train troops, but they could not be more different.

## GENERAL HUX

A young, ruthless officer in the First Order, General Hux has complete confidence in his troops, training methods, and weapons. He believes that peace in the galaxy can only be enforced by a strong hand. The son of a prominent Academy commandant from the Old Empire, Hux thinks it's his destiny to rise to the top of the First Order.

### INFO

| | |
|---|---|
| Homeworld | Arkanis |
| Affiliation | First Order |
| Species | Human |
| Height/weight | 1.85 meters/75 kilograms |
| Weapons | Sonn-Blas SE-44C officer's blaster pistol |
| Special move | Academy martial arts |

### STATS

| Intelligence | Strength | Agility | Damage | Control | Courage |
|---|---|---|---|---|---|
| 9 | 6 | 5.5 | 6 | 7 | 8.5 |

# THE SHOWDOWN

As a commando, Madine trained under the harshest conditions, slogging through swamps, jungles, and deserts. Hux, a keen strategist, has more experience with combat theory and attack planning. Now stranded in the deep, dark forests of Takodana, each must outmaneuver the other through the thick foliage to reach the single speeder bike.

## GENERAL MADINE

Formerly a member of an Imperial commando team, Crix Madine defected to the Rebel cause early in the Galactic Civil War. He brought valuable information regarding Imperial operations to the Alliance, earning the trust of High Command. By the time of the Empire's defeat, Madine was serving as commander of the Alliance Special Forces.

## STATS

| 7 | 7 | 5 | 6 | 7.5 | 10 |
|---|---|---|---|---|---|
| Intelligence | Strength | Agility | Damage | Control | Courage |

| | |
|---|---|
| Homeworld | Corellia |
| Affiliation | Rebel Alliance |
| Species | Human |
| Height/weight | 1.8 meters/82 kilograms |
| Weapons | BlasTech DH-17 blaster pistol |
| Special move | Corellian boxing |

INFO

**Who wins?**
See page 64.

# BOBBAJO  VS. MALAKILI

Neither of these opponents are combative by nature, but a disagreement over the care and feeding of flying xandus has caused Malakili to lose his temper. The sleepy-eyed Bobbajo seems more amused than startled by the slovenly rancor keeper.

## BOBBAJO

This creaky-jointed Nu-Cosian has a calm demeanor that helps settle down the mobile menagerie of jittery animals he carries in a stack of boxes atop his strong back. He is known to the settlers of Jakku as the crittermonger, for selling a wide variety of animals, as well as the storyteller, for spinning wild yarns.

## INFO

| | |
|---|---|
| Homeworld | Jakku |
| Affiliation | None |
| Species | Nu-Cosian |
| Height/weight | 1.14 meters/40 kilograms |
| Weapons | None |
| Special move | Unsettlingly unfazed |

## STATS

| Intelligence | Strength | Agility | Damage | Control | Courage |
|---|---|---|---|---|---|
| 7.5 | 4.5 | 2 | 3 | 3 | 7.5 |

# THE SHOWDOWN

Malakili holds his gaderffii stick over his head and mimics the growl of a Tusken Raider. Bobbajo blinks and begins to shuffle away. An incensed Malakili steps back to deliver an overhead blow when the sticky tongue of a worrt scavenger snaps out of a box on Bobbajo's back, disarming Malakili. The humiliated human clenches his meaty fists for another attack, only to be swarmed by a cloud of small humminghoppers from another of Bobbajo's boxes.

## MALAKILI

A former circus animal trainer who was later hired by Jabba the Hutt to tend to his rancor beast, Malakili is an antisocial, sour-faced thug who only shows tenderness and sympathy toward animals. He feels bad that the rancor's existence is a brutal one, and longs to one day escape with the beast.

## STATS

| Intelligence | Strength | Agility | Damage | Control | Courage |
|---|---|---|---|---|---|
| 7.5 | 4.5 | 2 | 3 | 3 | 7.5 |

**INFO**

| | |
|---|---|
| Homeworld | Tatooine |
| Affiliation | Criminal |
| Species | Human |
| Height/weight | 1.72 meters/95 kilograms |
| Weapons | Gaderffii (gaffi) stick |
| Special move | Gaffi stick clobber |

**Who wins?**
See page 64.

# UNKAR PLUTT (VS.) GAMORREAN GUARD

Sometimes fights get ugly, and sometimes fights *start* ugly. Unkar Plutt is the unsavory junk boss of Jakku, and not a scrap of salvage is sold or traded without his say-so. Plutt thinks a dim-witted Gamorrean has pocketed a shiny bauble from a junk pile without paying, so Unkar calls out the green-skinned brute.

## UNKAR PLUTT

Unkar runs a profitable business stealing, scavenging, and selling scrap on Jakku. He doles out slim servings of food in exchange for valuable salvage, and he calls upon leg-breakers and strong-arms to ensure he gets the best deals.

### INFO

| | |
|---|---|
| Homeworld | Jakku |
| Affiliation | Criminal |
| Species | Crolute |
| Height/weight | 1.8 meters/113 kilograms |
| Weapons | Unregistered snub blaster |
| Special move | Blob-hug holding move |

### STATS

| Intelligence | Strength | Agility | Damage | Control | Courage |
|---|---|---|---|---|---|
| 6 | 7.5 | 3.5 | 6 | 4 | 5.5 |

# THE SHOWDOWN

The junk boss bellows several choice insults at the Gamorrean. Most go over the pig guard's head, but when it dawns on the Gamorrean that he's being attacked, his beady little eyes focus on his Crolute combatant. He swings his cumbersome ax and misses but slices into a workbench.

## GAMORREAN GUARD

On their homeworld, Gamorreans live in clans led by powerful sow and warlord boars. Crafty crime lords, however, have pursuaded these dim-witted brutes to work cheaply as enforcers or bodyguards. Gamorreans prefer hand-to-hand combat or simple axes and bludgeons.

## STATS

| Intelligence | Strength | Agility | Damage | Control | Courage |
|:---:|:---:|:---:|:---:|:---:|:---:|
| 4 | 8 | 3 | 7 | 5 | 6 |

### INFO

| | |
|---|---|
| Homeworld | Gamorr |
| Affiliation | Criminal |
| Species | Gamorrean |
| Height/weight | Average 1.8 meters/100 kilograms |
| Weapons | Unpowered war ax |
| Special move | Overhead downward chop |

**Who wins?** See page 64.

History often repeats itself on the battlefield. When a Geonosian warrior from the aristocratic caste comes into conflict with a First Order incendiary assault trooper, jets of fire and sonic blasts fill the air along with echoes of the Clone Wars.

## FIRST ORDER FLAMETROOPER

Specialized stormtroopers of the First Order, flametroopers carry incendiary weapons that can transform any battlefield into a blazing inferno. The armored tanks on a flametrooper's back contain volatile conflagrine gel that is launched by a propellant gas and set ablaze by an igniter built into the double-barreled flamethrower projector gun.

## STATS

| Intelligence | Strength | Agility | Damage | Control | Courage |
|---|---|---|---|---|---|
| 5 | 7 | 5 | 7 | 6 | 8.5 |

### INFO

| | |
|---|---|
| Homeworld | Various |
| Affiliation | First Order |
| Species | Human |
| Height/weight | Average 1.83 meters/80 kilograms |
| Weapons | D-93 incinerator flamethrower |
| Special move | Wall of fire |

# THE SHOWDOWN

Within the confines of a Geonosian hive, the winged warrior is able to take advantage of the tall, vaulted ceilings to strike from above. The flametrooper's kit can launch a jet of fire about 75 meters, making the Geonosian in range even when close to the ceiling. Forced behind stone formations for cover, the insectoid combatant targets the trooper with a difficult-to-evade sonic blaster.

## GEONOSIAN WINGED WARRIOR

Although rendered extinct by the evil actions of the Galactic Empire, the winged warriors of the Geonosian aristocracy once proved to be a formidable opponent to the clone troopers of the Republic. Rumors persist that a few eggs have survived and perhaps a new hive will take root.

## STATS

| Intelligence | Strength | Agility | Damage | Control | Courage |
|:---:|:---:|:---:|:---:|:---:|:---:|
| 5 | 5 | 7 | 6 | 5 | 5 |

| | |
|---|---|
| **Homeworld** | Geonosis |
| **Affiliation** | Separatist Alliance |
| **Species** | Geonosians |
| **Height/weight** | 1.85 meters/64 kilograms |
| **Weapons** | Claws, Geonosian sonic blaster, electro-pike |
| **Special move** | Flutter charge |

INFO

**Who wins?**
See page 64.

## p. 4–5

### Luke Skywalker vs. Kylo Ren
**Winner: Kylo Ren**
Although Luke defends himself with intense determination, Kylo's anger overpowers the young Jedi. Despite injuries, Kylo is willing to press his advantage and defeat his enemy.

## p. 6–7

### Finn vs. MagnaGuard droid
**Winner: MagnaGuard**
The battered droid closes the distance to Finn and takes a swing. Finn parries a few blows with his blaster rifle, but the MagnaGuard lands a stunning, electrifying hit. If only Finn had a melee weapon handy!

## p. 8–9

### Rey vs. Tusken Raider
**Winner: Rey**
The Tusken Raider gets within reach and swings hard with his gaffi stick, but Rey blocks the blow with her staff. Spinning low, she sweeps the Tusken off his feet with her staff and goes in for a silencing blow.

## p. 10–11

### Poe Dameron vs. Aurra Sing
**Winner: Poe Dameron**
Although he sustains a few hits, Poe's courage and brashness win the day. He refuses to back down from Aurra's attempts at intimidation.

## p. 12–13

### BB-8 vs. Salacious B. Crumb
**Winner: BB-8**
Crumb's increasing frustration at his inability to grab hold of BB-8 gives the droid a chance to scorch the creature with a welding torch, sending the cowardly critter running.

## p. 14–15

### T-70 X-wing starfighter vs. TIE Advanced x1
**Winner: T-70 X-wing starfighter**
The Advanced x1 TIE is indeed maneuverable, spinning itself around while firing a steady stream of laser fire across the X-wing's path. But the T-70's shields and armor are too tough, and it is able to protect itself long enough to fire a decisive blow.

## p. 16–17

### Rathtar vs. Darth Vader
**Winner: Darth Vader**
Although the rathtar wraps Vader's body in its crushing grasp, the creature cannot stop the Sith Lord's mind. Vader crushes the rathtar's primitive brain with a telekinetic grip.

## p. 18–19

### Rey's speeder vs. Luke's landspeeder
**Winner: Luke's landspeeder**
Although Rey's speeder is swift and nimble, it can be difficult to steer. The driver is also more exposed when riding atop it. A good bump by another speeder, and he or she will be sent flying.

## p. 20–21

### Han Solo vs. Jango Fett
**Winner: Han Solo**
Having defeated Boba Fett, Han knows the bounty hunter's weak spot. Solo bides his time for the perfect shot then blasts Jango's jetpack, grounding the hunter for good.

## p. 22–23

### Chewbacca vs. Grummgar
**Winner: Chewbacca**
Hunting creatures has made Grummgar indifferent. He mistakes Chewbacca for just another dumb animal. Chewie's Wookiee convictions give him the extra boost to overpower his larger opponent.

## p. 24–25

### Special Forces TIE fighter vs. T-65 X-wing fighter
**Winner: Special Forces TIE fighter**
Although the X-wing puts up a good fight, it gets caught in the blast of a mag-pulse warhead. Its electronics are fried, making it easy prey for the TIE fighter's dedicated gunner.

## p. 26–27

### Teedo vs. Jawa
**Winner: Teedo**
The Teedo's spear makes contact with the Jawa's ionization blaster, sending a disabling jolt through the device. This effectively disarms the Jawa, giving the Teedo an unbeatable advantage.

## p. 28–29

### FO Star Destroyer vs. MC star cruiser
**Winner: First Order Star Destroyer**
In this case, size does matter. The MC80 doesn't stand a chance. It's too small to put a dent into the Star Destroyer, but too big to evade its withering cannon fire.

## p. 30–31

### First Order stormtrooper vs. clone trooper
**Winner: First Order stormtrooper**
Although both have comparable training, it's the stormtrooper that benefits from having studied the victories and losses of past armies. He is able to counter each of the clone trooper's tactics effectively.

## p. 32–33

### Happabore vs. Reek
**Winner: Reek**
Despite the happabore's size, the reek's increasing anger makes it victorious. One of its many repeated charges hits a soft spot in the happabore's hide, and the reek's deadly horn pierces the larger beast's flank.

## p. 34–35

### Millennium Falcon vs. Kylo Ren's shuttle
**Winner: Millennium Falcon**
As modern and advanced as the *Upsilon*-class shuttle is, it's no match for the ingenuity and reckless modifications wired into the *Falcon*'s design.

## p. 36–37

### Captain Phasma vs. Boba Fett
**Winner: Captain Phasma**
Phasma's rigid training keeps her in top physical form, and she is able to outlast Fett, enduring his attacks until his most potent weapon systems become depleted.

## p. 38–39

### TIE/FO fighter vs. Jedi starfighter
**Winner: Jedi starfighter**
The Delta-7 out-laps the TIE/FO fighter, snapping a shot that causes the First Order ship to career out of control.

## p. 40–41

### Snap Wexley vs. TIE fighter pilot
**Winner: Snap Wexley**
The burly Snap can take a punch. Despite the spry pilot's fast jabs, Snap grabs ahold of his opponent for the win.

## p. 42–43

### Constable Zuvio vs. Guavian security soldier
**Winner: Constable Zuvio**
Despite being outgunned, Zuvio refuses to give up. A well-timed throw of his hat severs the chemical reservoir that boosts the Guavian's strength and speed, allowing Zuvio to land a finishing blow.

## p. 44–45

### Tasu Leech vs. Aayla Secura
**Winner: Aayla Secura**
Although Tasu succeeds in disarming Aayla with an open-fist blow to her wrist, ultimately her superior combat training allows her to immobilize the nimble pirate.

## p. 46–47

### Bazine Netal vs. Zam Wesell
**Winner: Zam Wesell**
Bazine is a tough challenger, batting away many of Zam's weapons in close contact, but she has no defense against the sting of a centipede-like kouhun.

## p. 48–49

### First Order snowtrooper vs. Rebel commando
**Winner: Rebel commando**
At the last moment, the commando drops his cumbersome rifle, favoring his combat knife and fists. He ducks beneath the snowtrooper's fire and tackles the First Order soldier.

## p. 50–51

### General Leia Organa vs. General Veers
**Winner: General Leia Organa**
Veers underestimates Leia, thinking his youth, height, and physical prowess give him an advantage. But Leia has maintained her target practice and proves her superior skill.

## p. 52–53

### Captain Sidon Ithano vs. General Grievous
**Winner: General Grievous**
Both warriors rely on a certain amount of bluster, but it is Grievous who has more fight behind his bark.

## p. 54–55

### First Order snowspeeder vs. AAT assault tank
**Winner: AAT assault tank**
The snowspeeder is able to race circles around the slower tank, but its antipersonnel weapon has no hope of cracking the thick shell protecting the AAT crew. The tank gunners simply have to wait for one of their shots to land and it's all over.

## p. 56–57

### General Hux vs. General Madine
**Winner: General Madine**
Ultimately, Madine fails to fall into the classical patterns that Hux has studied, and he surprises the young general.

## p. 58–59

### Bobbajo vs. Malakili
**Winner: Bobbajo**
After getting hounded by Bobbajo's steelpeckers, zhhee, gwerps, and pishnes, Malakili surrenders and comes to respect Bobbajo's animal-training skills.

## p. 60–61

### Unkar Plutt vs. Gamorrean guard
**Winner: Unkar Plutt**
Plutt still packs a punch even though he spends most of his days sitting behind a counter. Far smarter than the Gamorrean, he easily distracts the guard by pointing at a nonexistent threat and then throws sand into the guard's eyes.

## p. 62–63

### FO flametrooper vs. Geonosian winged warrior
**Winner: First Order flametrooper**
History repeats itself. The Geonosians are simply no match for a flamethrower-wielding trooper.